Alison Holst's Chocolate Temptations

Everyday Treats & Occasional Indulgences

First published 1996 by
Hyndman Publishing
PO Box 5017, Dunedin
ISBN 0-9583401-6-1

© Text: Alison Holst
Designer: Rob Di Leva
Production: Di Leva Design
Illustrator: Clare Ferguson
Photography: Sal Criscillo
Home Economists: Alison Holst,
Jane Ritchie, Dee Harris
Printing: Tablet Colour Print
2nd Reprint October 1997

All rights reserved. No part of this publication may be produced, stored in a retrieval system, or transmitted in any form, or by means electronic, mechanical, photocopying, recording or otherwise, without prior permission in writing of the publisher.

The recipes in this book have been carefully tested by the author. The publisher and the author have made every effort to ensure that the instructions are accurate and safe, but they cannot accept liability for any resulting injury or loss or damage to property whether direct or consequential. Because ovens and microwave ovens vary so much, you should use the cooking times suggested in recipes as guides only. The first time you make a recipe, check it at intervals to make sure it is not cooking faster, or more slowly than expected.

Always follow the detailed instructions given by the manufacturers of your appliances and equipment, rather than the more general instructions given in these recipes.

COVER PHOTOGRAPH:
Chocolate Orange Liqueur Cake (Page 8)

Contents

Weights and Measures	4
Cooking with Chocolate	5
Chocolate Icings	6
Celebration Cakes	8
Family Favourite Chocolate Cakes	10
Chocolate Slices and Squares	20
Coffee Time Temptations	22
Children's Treats	28
Everyday and Lunchbox Cookies	30
Chocolate Muffins	34
Warming Winter Puddings	35
Cold Chocolate Desserts	39
Luscious Chocolate Pies	46
Sumptuous Chocolate Sauces	48
Chocolate Fondue	50
Fabulous Chocolate Fudge	53
Tempting Truffles	54
Homemade Chocolates	56
Chocolate Dipped Delights	58
Chocolate Decorations	59
Hot and Cold Chocolate Drinks	60
Index	62

Important Information

To get successful results each time you cook, you need to work systematically.

Before you start, read the recipe through carefully, from beginning to end, and make sure that you understand what you are meant to do.

Make sure you have all the food and equipment you need, before you start cooking. If everything you need is out before you start, your cooking time will be shorter and more fun. (My cooking on television looks easy because everything is out, ready to use, before I put everything together!)

Measure ingredients carefully, so you get the results the recipe writer intended.

Use standard metric measuring cups (1 cup holds 250mls) and metric measuring spoons for the recipes in this book.-

1 teaspoon holds 5 ml
1 tablespoon holds 15 ml
1 cup holds about 16 tablespoons

All the cup and spoon measures are level unless otherwise stated. (Rounded or heaped measures upset the balance of dry and liquid measures.)

When measuring flour, stir it round with a fork, then spoon it lightly into the cup without shaking or banging it. Level off the top with the back of a straight knife. ¼ and ½ cup measures save you time if you are doing a lot of baking. If flour is packed down, you will be using more than the recipe intends.

Most butter quantities are given by weight. Small amounts are measured by tablespoon. 1 tablespoonful weighs 15 grams.

½ cup chocolate chips weighs about 100g

Brown sugar is measured by packing it into a cup or spoon so that it holds its shape like a sand castle when turned out.

Golden syrup is measured in rounded household tablespoons which have been heated in hot water.

Large eggs are used in all recipes, unless otherwise stated.

| cm | centimetre | °C | degrees Celcius |
| g | gram | ml | millilitre |

Microwave cooking times are variable, and are meant as a guide only. I use a 720 watt microwave with a turntable.

High	100% power
Medium-High	70% power
Medium	50% power
Defrost	30% power

Acknowledgements

ALISON'S CHOICE for dried fruit, nuts and selected baking ingredients

BARKERS FRUIT PROCESSORS LTD for preserves

BENNICKS POULTRY FARM, Levin for fresh eggs

EMPIRE FOODSTUFFS for spices

HARKNESS AND YOUNG LTD for Probus utensils and Willow non-stick cookware

J. WATTIE FOODS for canned fruit

LAMNEI PLASTICS, Lower Hutt for Alison Holst's Microwave Dishes

S.C. JOHNSON & SON PTY LTD for Chef Mate

SUREBRAND for Teflon liners

TUI FOODS LTD for Tararua dairy products

Cooking with Chocolate

Chocolate must surely be the most popular flavour around! Cooking with chocolate, you can both please your family with "goodies" as affordable weekday treats, and make festive occasions memorable with extra-special masterpieces!

This book contains my family's favourite chocolate recipes. I hope that you will find them just as popular.

You can use cocoa or chocolate to get a chocolate flavour.

The cocoa used in this book is "plain" cocoa, not the darker, "Dutch Process" cocoa, which has a stronger, slightly different flavour.

When you make the recipes which call for chocolate, you can use one of a number of different chocolate products.

You can use dark, milk or white chocolate bars which are normally bought for eating. (Dark chocolate is usually preferred for cooking.) You may also use bars labelled "cooking chocolate", or other bars or small shapes labelled for specific purposes, such as "easy to melt".

If you can't decide what chocolate to use for a recipe, I suggest that you try chocolate chips. I have found that they work well for many purposes. They are easier to hide from your family than blocks of chocolate, are easily measured, melted, and do not require chopping up.

Melting Chocolate

Take care when melting chocolate. A small amount of water can prevent chocolate melting to a smooth glossy mixture. Do not cover chocolate when melting it, or water may drip in from the lid. Always stir with a dry spoon.

If the melting chocolate turns dull and grainy, you must start again with more chocolate. (Have extra on hand.)

Do not heat chocolate more than necessary, while melting it.

Melt chocolate, in small, even pieces, in a glass, stainless steel or china bowl over or in pot or pan of hot water.

I usually melt block chocolate on my stove, but sometimes microwave chocolate chips on Medium power, stirring them every 30 seconds. (Microwaved chocolate keeps its shape, until stirred.)

If there are melting instructions on the chocolate you use, follow them! For dipping and decorating see pages 58 & 59.

Leftover melted chocolate which has hardened may be remelted later.

Different brands and types of chocolate, and different room temperatures and humidity will affect melting times, so watch carefully, rather than using specific times.

Cocoa Based Icings

*These traditional chocolate icings are made with cocoa and icing sugar.
Heating the cocoa, or using boiling water, makes the colour darker and the flavour richer.*

Everyday Chocolate Icing

1 Tbsp cocoa
1½ Tbsp boiling water
2 tsp butter
¼ tsp vanilla
1 cup icing sugar

Put the cocoa in a small bowl. Pour on boiling water and mix to a paste. Add room-temperature butter, vanilla and sifted icing sugar, then beat until smooth and thick. Add a little extra water or icing sugar to adjust thickness if necessary.

Spread on cake or slice etc, using a knife or spatula.

Chocolate Glaze

2 Tbsp cocoa
¼ cup water
½ tsp vanilla
1 cup icing sugar

This makes a firm, dark, shiny glaze. Heat the cocoa and water together in a small container. As soon as the mixture thickens and begins to look dry, remove from the heat and stir in vanilla.

Cool container until you can touch the bottom with your hand. Stir in half the sifted icing sugar. Like magic the dryish chocolate mixture will turn into a thin, dark brown shiny mixture. Add enough of the remaining icing sugar to make the glaze the thickness you want.

Dip the tops of chocolate eclairs into the mixture.

Mocha Icing

1 tsp instant coffee
2 Tbsp cocoa
2 Tbsp boiling water
1 Tbsp butter
1½ cups icing sugar

Stir the coffee and cocoa together in a small bowl. Mix to a paste with the boiling water. Add the room-temperature butter and the sifted icing sugar and beat until smooth. Add more water or icing sugar until you get a good spreading consistency. Spread on cake or slice etc, using a knife or spatula.

Chocolate Based Icings

If you have trouble with cocoa based icings try these! They are based on chocolate, are easy to mix and always have a good flavour and colour.

Sour Cream Chocolate Icing

50g dark, milk or white chocolate, chocolate melts or ¼ cup chocolate chips
2 Tbsp sour cream

This mixture never hardens completely.

Break up chocolate, if necessary, and heat with sour cream over boiling water or in a microwave until the chocolate has melted. Stir until well combined.

Cool to spreadable consistency if necessary. Spread on cakes or slices.

Variation: For a biscuit icing which sets hard, use half the amount of sour cream, i.e. 1 tablespoon.

Cream Cheese Chocolate Icing

50g dark chocolate, chocolate melts or ¼ cup chocolate chips
½ cup (125g) cream cheese
3 Tbsp icing sugar

Break the chocolate into pieces, if necessary, and melt in a bowl over boiling water or in a microwave oven.

Beat the cream cheese and icing sugar together in a food processor, or by hand, until smooth. Add the melted chocolate and process or stir until completely mixed.

Mixture thickens as it cools, but never hardens completely. Spread on cake when cool.

Variation: For white icing, (e.g. for Carrot Cake) use 50g of white chocolate.

Note: Double quantities for a large cake.

Chocolate Liqueur Icing

125g dark cooking chocolate
100g butter
1–2 Tbsp orange liqueur

Break the chocolate into pieces, and heat with the other ingredients in a small heatproof bowl over a small pot of boiling water.

Stir the mixture until the chocolate has melted and all ingredients are evenly mixed.

Cool to spreadable consistency then spread evenly on cake using a knife or spatula.

Variation: Use brandy or rum to replace the orange liqueur.

Chocolate Orange Liqueur Cake

Make this wonderful cake to celebrate a very special occasion! It owes its outstanding texture to a high proportion of dark chocolate and ground almonds. A 20cm cake will make 8–10 servings. You can freeze the second cake, or halve the recipe if you like.

For 1 23cm or 2 20cm round cakes:

250g dark cooking chocolate
¼ cup orange liqueur
rind of 1 orange
1 cup caster sugar
250g butter, softened
6 large eggs, separated
¼ tsp citric acid
1 tsp water
1 cup ground almonds
¾ cup flour

Icing:

125g dark cooking chocolate
100g butter
1–2 Tbsp orange liqueur

Break the chocolate into pieces of even size. Melt it with the liqueur in a bowl over a pot of hot water, stirring until well combined. Put aside to cool.

Peel the orange with a potato peeler. Put the rind in a food processor bowl with three quarters of the caster sugar and process until very finely chopped. Add the softened, but not melted butter, process until light and fluffy, then beat in the egg yolks and the citric acid dissolved in the water. Add the cooled chocolate mixture, then the ground almonds and flour, and lightly mix.

In another bowl, beat the egg whites until they form soft peaks. Add the remaining caster sugar and beat until mixture forms peaks which turn over when you lift the beater. Do not overbeat. Carefully fold the chocolate mixture through the beaten egg whites.

Line bottom and sides of 1 23cm or 2 20cm round baking tins with baking paper or Teflon liner(s). Pour the mixture into the tin(s) and bake at 180°C for about 45 minutes for a 23cm cake and about 30–40 minutes for the 20cm cakes, until centre feels as firm as the edges, and a skewer pushed into the middle of the cake comes out clean. Leave for 10 minutes before turning out onto a wire rack.

Icing: Combine all ingredients and heat in a bowl over hot water until melted. Mix well. Cool before spreading on cake.

Decorate as desired. (For chocolate shavings see page 59.)

Variations: Replace orange liqueur with rum or brandy. Leave out orange rind, citric acid and water if desired.

This cake is photographed on the front cover.

Chocolate Soufflé Roll

This "Special Occasion" sponge roll is made with plenty of eggs, and with cocoa instead of flour. The result is extra-soft and moist, whether it is filled with plain whipped cream or the rich chocolate cream filling given here.

For 6–8 servings:

Roll:

6 large eggs
pinch of salt
½ cup sugar
½ cup cocoa

Chocolate Filling:

200g cooking chocolate
2 Tbsp rum
250–300g cream

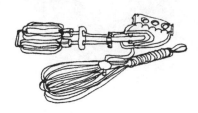

Separate eggs, putting whites in a large bowl and yolks in a smaller one. Beat the whites with the salt until they form peaks with tips that turn over when the beater is lifted out. Add half the sugar and beat again, to the same stage. (Do not overbeat.)

Without washing the beater, beat the egg yolks and the remaining sugar until thick and foamy (but not as stiff as the whites). Sift the cocoa several times and put aside in the sieve. Fold the yolks into the whites by hand, using a spatula. When mixed, sieve the cocoa evenly over the top and fold in until evenly dispersed.

Spread mixture evenly in a large (23 x 35cm) sponge roll tin lined with baking paper or a Teflon liner and bake at 160°C for 15–20 minutes, or until the centre springs back when pressed and a toothpick pushed into the centre comes out clean. (If mixture wrinkles and deflates, it has cooked too long.)

Turn out onto a clean teatowel sprinkled with 2 tablespoons of sifted cocoa. Roll up immediately, incorporating the teatowel in the roll. Unroll when cold, carefully remove teatowel, spread with whipped cream or chocolate filling and re-roll.

Refrigerate for at least an hour, before serving.

Chocolate Filling: Break up the chocolate and heat over hot water with the rum until the chocolate has melted. Add 2 tablespoons of the cream and stir until smooth. Cool.

Whip remaining cream until firm, then fold in the cooled chocolate mixture. Refrigerate until ready to fill the roll.

Chocolate Applecake

This cake is versatile! It is just as popular served with coffee as it is packed in lunch boxes. If you don't feel energetic enough to make the crunchy topping just decorate your applecake with slivered almonds before you cook it.

For a 23cm cake:

Crunchy Topping:

¼ cup brown sugar
2 Tbsp flour
1 tsp cinnamon
25g cold butter
2 Tbsp chopped walnuts

Alternative Topping:

¼ cup slivered almonds

Cake:

2–3 apples
125g butter, melted
1 large egg
1 cup sugar
1½ cups flour
2 Tbsp cocoa
1 tsp cinnamon
1 tsp baking soda

Prepare the topping in a food processor, using the metal chopping blade to chop everything briefly, or rub the ingredients together by hand. Put aside.

Chop unpeeled apples in the (unwashed) food processor (or grate them into a bowl). Add remaining ingredients in the order given, sieving the last four ingredients onto the others if mixing by hand. Mix briefly, until ingredients are combined. (Always check baking soda for lumps by pressing it with a spoon against the palm of your hand before adding it with other ingredients.)

Turn mixture into a 23cm square or round pan lined with baking paper or coated with non-stick spray, as this mixture sticks easily! Sprinkle with prepared topping or with slivered almonds.

Bake at 190°C for about 25–30 minutes or until the centre springs back when pressed. Cool in the pan for a few minutes before turning out.

Serve with whipped cream or icecream.

Chocolate Zucchini Cake

This unusual combination of ingredients makes a really delicious, large, moist, family cake which you can serve with pride. This recipe is especially useful for zucchini growers!

For a 25cm square cake:

125g butter, softened
1 cup brown sugar
¾ cup white sugar
3 large eggs
2 ½ cups flour
1 tsp vanilla
½ cup yoghurt, plain or flavoured
¼ cup cocoa
2 tsp baking soda
1 tsp cinnamon
½ tsp mixed spice
½ tsp salt
3 cups (350g) grated zucchini
½ – 1 cup chocolate chips or pieces

Line a 25cm square cake tin or roasting pan with two crosswise strips of baking paper.

Beat the butter with the sugars in a food processor or electric beater until light and creamy. Add the eggs one at a time, adding a little of the measured flour with each egg to prevent the mixture curdling, and beating well after each addition. Add the vanilla and yoghurt and mix well.

Put aside ½ cup of the measured flour and sift the rest with the other dry ingredients. Mix the grated zucchini into the egg mixture. Fold the sifted dry ingredients into the egg mixture without overmixing. The final mixture should be just wet enough to pour into the tin. If it seems too runny, fold in part, or all of the reserved ½ cup of flour. (A cake with less flour is softer.)

Turn into the prepared pan. Sprinkle the surface with the chocolate chips.

Bake at 170°C preferably without the fan, for 30 – 45 minutes, or until the centre feels firm and a skewer comes out clean. Cut when cold.

Store in the refrigerator up to 3 days.

Mississippi Mud Cake

Don't you think that this is a wonderful name for a dense, dark chocolate cake? In my mind's eye I see hippopotamuses wallowing in semi-liquid mud, even though I know they are not one of the Mississippi's attractions!

For a 23cm ring cake, about 8 servings:

1 Tbsp instant coffee
½ cup water
100g dark cooking chocolate or chocolate chips
100g butter
1 cup sugar
2 Tbsp sherry, whisky or brandy
2 large eggs
1 tsp vanilla
1¼ cups flour
½ tsp baking soda

Heat the instant coffee, water, broken up chocolate, butter and sugar until the chocolate has melted and the sugar dissolved, stirring at intervals if microwaving, and all the time if heating on the stove top. Cool to room temperature, stir in sherry or spirits.

Beat the eggs with the vanilla in a food processor or bowl.

Sift the flour and baking soda together, then combine the three mixtures. Process or whisk just long enough to get a smooth mixture which is thinner than most cake mixtures.

Line the bottom of a ring tin (which will hold at least 6 cups) with baking paper, or a non-stick Teflon liner, and butter or spray its sides carefully. Pour cake mixture into the prepared tin, and bake at 150°C for about an hour, or until the sides of the cake shrink away from the sides of the cake tin, and a skewer in the thickest part of the cake comes out clean.

Leave to cool in the tin for about 10 minutes, then run a knife around the sides as a precaution, and invert onto its serving plate.

Serve dusted with icing sugar, with icecream or lightly whipped, chilled cream, and a dribble of coffee flavoured liqueur if you like.

Mississippi Mud Cake

Banana Chocolate Cake

Chocolate Banana Cake

This cake is moist, soft, and well-flavoured, with a light texture. It is lovely eaten slightly warm, before it cools, and should be finished within a couple of days. I don't think you will find this difficult!

For 2 23 x 10cm loaves
or 1 23cm ring cake:

200g butter, soft but not melted
1½ cups sugar
1 tsp vanilla
2 large eggs
1 cup (about 2) ripe mashed bananas
½ cup buttermilk or ½ cup milk with
    1 tsp wine vinegar
2 cups flour
3 Tbsp cocoa
1 tsp baking powder
¾ tsp baking soda

Mix the butter, sugar and vanilla until fluffy. Add the eggs one at a time, beating well after each addition.

Mash and measure the banana and mix with the buttermilk or the milk and vinegar. If using a food processor, pour this mixture on top of the cake mixture, then measure on top of all of it all the dry ingredients. Process in brief bursts to mix the banana mixture and dry ingredients through the creamed mixture. If mixing any other way, sift the dry ingredients together, then fold half the banana mixture and half the sifted mixture through cake with a spatula or rubber scraper. Repeat with the remaining halves. Stop mixing as soon as everything is combined.

Bake in two 23 x 10cm loaf tins each lined with a strip of baking paper going across the long sides and the bottom.

The mixture is rather big for a 23cm ring pan, but it works well and makes an attractive cake if you make the sides higher using strips of baking paper stuck in place with a little butter. Line the bottom of the ring pan with paper, too.

Bake the loaves and the ring cake at 180°C for 30–40 minutes, or until a skewer in the middle comes out clean and the centre springs back when pressed.

Dust the top with icing sugar before serving, or ice with Everday Chocolate Icing from page 6 or Sour Cream Chocolate Icing from page 7, when cold. Do not store the iced cake in a sealed tin, or the top may become sticky.

Family Cakes

When you are cooking for children it is a help to have a few favourite recipes up your sleeve...

Three Minute Chocolate Sponge

A popular "all in together" cake!

For a 20cm cake or a 23cm ring cake:
75g butter, melted
3 large eggs
¾ cup sugar
2 Tbsp milk
1 cup flour, minus 2 Tbsp
2 tsp baking powder
2 Tbsp cocoa

Melt the butter in a bowl which will hold the whole mixture. Add the eggs, sugar and milk to the melted butter.

Sift in the carefully measured flour, baking powder and cocoa.

Using an electric beater or a good hand beater, beat until the mixture is well mixed, looks creamy and is slightly paler in colour, about 30–60 seconds.

Turn into a 20 cm square or round cake tin, or a ring tin, lined with baking paper or a Teflon non-stick liner. (Butter or spray uncovered sides.) Bake at 175°C for about 20 minutes or until the centre springs back when pressed.

Dust with icing sugar or ice when cold, using a suitable recipe from pages 6 and 7.

Variation: For Jaffa cake add finely grated rind of one orange and replace 1 tablespoon milk with 1 tablespoon orange juice.

Kirsten's Chocolate Cake

My daughter uses this recipe often, to make excellent layer cakes, and birthday cakes of all shapes and sizes.

125g butter
2 rounded household Tbsp golden syrup
2 large eggs
2 cups flour
2 Tbsp cocoa
2 tsp baking powder
2 tsp baking soda
1 cup sugar
1½ cups milk

Warm the butter and golden syrup until just melted. Stir to combine.

Put the remaining ingredients, in the order given, in a food processor. Mix in

Family Cakes

...See which of these "family" chocolate cakes you find most popular and reliable.

brief bursts, then add the golden syrup and butter mixture, and process for two thirty second bursts.

Bake in two 20cm round tins (with high sides) if you want a cream-filled sandwich cake or intend to make a four-layered cake. For a rectangular, unfilled cake, bake in a large rectangular pan about 22cm x 27cm with rounded corners. Line tins with baking paper or a Teflon liner.

Bake at 180°C for 25 minutes, or until centre springs back when pressed, and a skewer in the centre comes out clean. Ice with chocolate icing from pages 6 and 7.

This cake is best the day it is made although it will last for 3 days.

Note: Some people have great success with this recipe, but others do not produce such good results. I do not know why!

Crazy Cake

This cake works despite containing no eggs, butter or milk. It doesn't even need a beater!

For a 20cm round or ring cake:

1½ cups flour
2 Tbsp cocoa
1 tsp cinnamon
1 tsp ginger
1 tsp baking soda
1 tsp salt
1 cup sugar
½ cup oil
2 Tbsp vinegar
1 tsp vanilla
¾ cup water

Line a 20cm square or ring tin with a layer of baking paper or a non-stick liner.

Measure the first six ingredients and sift together into a fairly large bowl. Add the sugar and toss to mix in with the other ingredients.

Measure the oil and add to the dry ingredients without stirring in. Add the vinegar, vanilla and water, and stir well with a fork until smooth.

Pour the mixture into the prepared tin and bake at 190°C for 30–40 minutes until the centre of the cake springs back when pressed or until a skewer comes out clean. Leave the cake in the tin for 4–5 minutes, then turn out on a wire rack and leave to cool.

Dust with sieved icing sugar or ice with Everyday Icing from page 6 or Sour Cream Chocolate Icing from page 7.

Kirsten's Chocolate Roll

For years this was the only cake my daughter ever wanted for her birthday. I found it easy and reliable to make as long as I measured everything accurately and did not let it overcook!

3 large eggs
½ cup sugar
½ cup flour
2 Tbsp cocoa
1 tsp baking powder
1 Tbsp boiling water

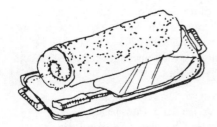

Using an electric beater beat together the eggs and sugar until the mixture is thick, creamy and has turned pale. (For the best results use room temperature eggs.)

Measure the flour, cocoa and baking powder into a sieve over the bowl, shake over the egg mixture then fold in carefully but thoroughly until no lumps of dry ingredients remain, using a spatula. Add the boiling water and fold again.

Line the bottom and two sides of a fairly large (about 22 x 30cm) sponge roll tin with baking paper and spread the mixture evenly.

Bake at 230°C (or 220°C in a fan oven) for 7–10 minutes or until the centre springs back when pressed lightly with a finger. (Take care not to cook longer than necessary or the roll will shrink.)

Working quickly, loosen the sponge from the unlined sides of the tin and turn out onto a clean tea towel that has been wet, then rung out as dry as possible. Lift off the baking paper and roll the sponge and tea towel up together, lightly but firmly. (Roll either way, depending on whether a short thick roll, or a long thin one is required.)

Stand the roll wrapped in the towel on a rack until it is cold. Unroll carefully, spread with raspberry jam and freshly whipped cream and roll up again — this time without the tea towel!

Dust with icing sugar just before serving.

Aunt Lucy's Mistake

Aunt Lucy is not a relation of mine, but she was the much loved aunt of a friend. Once, in an absent-minded moment, she muddled up a recipe while baking. The resulting cake was better than the original, and is always called Aunt Lucy's Mistake.

For a 20–23cm cake:

1 cup sugar
3 large eggs
200g butter, softened
¼ cup cocoa
¼ cup boiling water
1½ cups (200g) flour
2 tsp baking powder
1 cup desiccated coconut
½ cup milk

Measure the sugar and eggs into a food processor bowl and process until thick and creamy. Gradually add the softened, but not melted butter and mix until well combined.

Measure the cocoa into a cup or small bowl, add the boiling water and stir until mixed. Put in the food processor and without mixing add the flour and baking powder. Process briefly to mix in the cocoa and flour. Do not overmix. Add the coconut and milk and process again until just combined.

If you use an electric mixer, use the usual creaming method for the butter, sugar and eggs, beat in the cocoa mixture before you fold in the sifted flour and baking powder, then stir in the coconut and milk at the end.

Prepare a 20–23cm cake tin by lining with baking paper or a Teflon liner. Pour cake mixture into prepared tin.

Bake at 180°C for about 30 minutes, depending on the tin size. The cake is cooked when it starts to shrink at the edge and springs back in the middle.

Ice with Everyday Chocolate Icing from page 6.

Popular Chocolate Slices

*Slices seem easier to make than biscuits which must be individually shaped.
They keep well too — if you can find a really good hiding place.*

Brownies

Brownies are American favourites, loved for their dense fudgy texture, as well as their no-fuss preparation. They need no icing, and freeze well, too.

125g butter
1 cup sugar
2 large eggs
1 tsp vanilla
1 cup less 1 Tbsp flour (100g)
5 Tbsp cocoa
1 tsp baking powder
½ cup chopped walnuts, optional

Mix the brownies in a medium-sized pot. Melt the butter until it is liquid but not hot. Remove from the heat and beat in with a fork the sugar, eggs, and vanilla. Sift in the flour, cocoa and baking powder. Stir these in with the chopped nuts, if used.

Pour mixture into a 20–23cm square tin lined with baking paper. Smooth the surface.

Bake at 180°C for 30 minutes, or until firm in the centre. Mixture will rise up and sink again. The edges will probably be a little higher than the middle. When cold, cut into rectangles.

Serve as is, or roll in sifted icing sugar just before serving, covering all surfaces. Brownies do not require icing.

Nice with tea or coffee, or with icecream for dessert.

Fudge Squares

Teach your children how to make these easy unbaked, crumb-based squares. In warm weather hide them in the fridge and enjoy them chilled.

75g butter
½ cup brown sugar
3 Tbsp milk
¼ cup cocoa
250g packet Malt or Digestive biscuits, finely crushed
¾ –1 cup chopped walnuts
1 tsp vanilla

Bring the butter, sugar, milk and cocoa to the boil in a medium-sized pot, stirring constantly. Remove from the heat and add the crushed biscuits, chopped nuts and flavouring.

Popular Chocolate Slices

*On these two pages are three squares with very different textures.
See which becomes a family favourite in your house.*

Press mixture into a sponge roll tin (you do not have to fill the tin) until it is the size and depth you like. Flatten surface with the back of a spoon.

Ice with Everyday Chocolate Icing from page 6 or Sour Cream Icing from page 7. Cut into small squares when firm.

Variations: Add peppermint essence to both the base and icing. Use finely grated tangelo or orange rind in the base and/or the icing for a jaffa flavour. Replace the walnuts with lightly toasted almonds and flavour the icing with almond essence. Add rum essence to the base and icing instead of or as well as the vanilla.

Chocolate Lunch Box Squares

I find these squares are irresistible as long as the base is not overcooked. Time the baking carefully, since I know of no other way to tell when the base is ready.

For 20–30 pieces:

150g butter
¼ cup golden syrup
1 cup sugar
1½ cups flour
1 Tbsp cocoa
2 cups malted wheatflakes
½ cup sultanas

Melt the butter and golden syrup together in a saucepan or microwave container. Add the sugar and stir until well mixed.

Sift the flour and cocoa and add with the wheatflakes and sultanas to the butter mixture. Fold together until combined.

Press the mixture into a 23cm square cake tin which has been lightly buttered, sprayed with non-stick spray or lined with baking paper or a Teflon liner.

Bake at 160°C for 20 minutes.

Allow to cool slightly before icing with Everyday Chocolate Icing from page 6 or Sour Cream Icing from page 7. Cut into squares when cold.

Store in an airtight container.

Little Lava Rocks

These delicious, rich little "rocks" have a special texture and a spectacular mottled appearance. I tried to make a smaller mixture, but this was too hard. Don't worry about making too many — I hate to tell you how fast these disappear in our house!

For 80 little rocks:

250g dark chocolate
100g butter
½ cup caster sugar
1 tsp vanilla
3 large eggs
1¼ cups plain flour
¼ cup self-raising flour
¼ cup cocoa
about 1 cup icing sugar

Break the chocolate into even sized squares and heat gently with the cubed butter, over low heat, in a fairly large pot, stirring often, until you have a smooth mixture. Do not heat the mixture any more than necessary.

Remove from the heat and beat in the sugar and vanilla, then the eggs, one at a time, with a wooden spoon or spatula.

Put a sieve over the bowl and measure the flours and cocoa into it. Sift them into the chocolate mixture. Mix again, until well combined.

Chill mixture for a few minutes in a freezer or longer in a refrigerator, until firm enough to roll into balls.

Sift the icing sugar into a large round flat-bottomed dry bowl. (Unsifted icing sugar will not coat the biscuits well).

Divide the mixture into quarters and form each part into 20 little balls, using your hands. Drop four or five balls at a time into the icing sugar and rotate the bowl until the balls are thickly coated. Without brushing off any icing sugar, place the balls on baking trays covered with baking paper or Teflon liners. Leave at least 5cm between each one.

Bake at 170°C for about 10 minutes, until centres feel soft and springy when you touch them. Rocks will have spread slightly and will have a cracked surface if you used enough icing sugar. Handle and store carefully to stop the icing sugar from smudging.

Little Lava Rocks and Chocolate Dipped Hearts (see page 31)

Neenish Tarts and Chocolate Caramel Bars (see page 26)

Neenish Tarts

Neenish tarts are not made in a matter of moments. Even so, occasionally, I make a batch, because I love their combination of flavours and textures, and because I have never bought a Neenish tart which comes up to my expectations!

Tart shells:

100g butter
¾ cup icing sugar
1 cup flour
½ cup cornflour
milk, if necessary

Filling:

1 tsp gelatine
1 Tbsp water
50g butter
½ cup icing sugar
2 Tbsp warm water
¼ – ½ tsp rum essence

Cream the butter and icing sugar until light. Stir in the flour and cornflour. (If mixture is too crumbly to press into a dough add milk to dampen.) Form into a cylinder about 6cm in diameter and chill for 15 minutes to firm up. Slice the chilled dough into 3mm thick rounds, and press evenly into shallow, well sprayed patty tins. Prick with a fork.

Bake at 170°C for 10 minutes or until they darken slightly. Cool briefly in the tins, rotate carefully to ensure they have not stuck, then lift onto a rack to cool.

To make the filling sprinkle the gelatine onto cold water, leave to soften for 2–3 minutes, then heat briefly to dissolve. Cool.

In a food processor mix together the softened butter and icing sugar. Blend in the warm water and essence before adding the cooled gelatine. Process to combine. Chill until cold but not set hard.

Fill the cooked tart shells with the chilled filling and level off with the back of the knife blade.

You need to make two icings for Neenish Tarts. Make half the recipe of Everyday Chocolate Icing from page 6 then make the white icing by mixing in a bowl half cup icing sugar, one tablespoon room temperature butter and about two teaspoons hot water.

To ice the tarts, cover half the filled shell with the chocolate icing then refrigerate. Use a straight knife blade to ensure that the edge between the two icings is straight, then cover the rest of the surface in the same way with the white icing. Leave to set before storing in the refrigerator.

Chocolate Caramel Bars

Sometimes, when somebody goes out to buy the ingredients we need for our next cooking project, they come back with a small treat from a nearby baker's shop! When you make these yourself, you get a whole batch for the same price as two bought pieces!

Crust:

100g butter
¼ cup caster sugar
1 cup flour

Filling:

100g butter
½ of a 400g can sweetened condensed milk
½ cup golden syrup
¼ cup chopped walnuts

Cream the softened butter and the caster sugar, then stir in the flour. Press into a sponge roll tin that has been lined with a non-stick Teflon liner, or baking paper. (The size of the tin is not critical. A smaller tin makes a deeper bar.)

Bake at 170°C for 6–8 minutes or until the centre is firm. Do not overcook, or your bars will be very hard to cut later.

To make the filling, measure the butter, condensed milk, and golden syrup into a pot. Bring to the boil over medium heat, stirring all the time, then reduce the heat and cook for 10 minutes, stirring often, until the mixture is a deep golden colour, and a drop of it forms a soft ball in cold water.

Remove from the heat, stir in the chopped walnuts, and pour over the cooked base straight away, smoothing it out if necessary. Leave to cool before icing.

Make Everyday Chocolate Icing from page 6 adding a little extra water so it is easy to spread on the caramel. Leave uncovered for at least two hours before cutting into rectangles.

See photograph on page 24.

Chocolate Lamingtons

Lamingtons are always popular with both adults and children. They are very easy to make and even young children love to help with them. Freeze what you do not plan to eat in the next day or so.

For 24 or 25 Lamingtons:
500g bought unfilled sponge
¼ cup cocoa
½ cup water
¼ cup raspberry jam
¾ cup hot water
2 cups icing sugar
about 1½ cups fine coconut

Cut the sponge into 24 - 25 cubes. I like to cut off the brown top before I do this as it soaks up the syrup better, but this is not essential.

Measure the cocoa and the first measure of water into a small pot or microwave jug. Stir thoroughly to make sure there are no lumps, then boil until the colour darkens and the mixture thickens.

Add the jam, stir again and bring back to the boil. Add the hot water then stir in the icing sugar, making a fairly thin mixture, which will coat the sponge evenly. It will not be completely smooth, and can be strained, but I do not think this is really necessary.

Dip the sponge cubes one by one into the chocolate syrup, turning to coat evenly. Flick to remove excess icing, then turn in the coconut. I find the best way to do this is to put about ¼ cup of coconut into a plastic bag, or a lidded plastic bowl. Shake, making sure you enclose some air in the plastic bag. Leave lamingtons to dry on a cake rack. (If you put too much coconut in the container at a time it tends to discolour.)

Store in airtight containers. Keep in the refrigerator up to 2 days or freeze.

To serve, split and fill with a teaspoonful of raspberry jam and whipped cream.

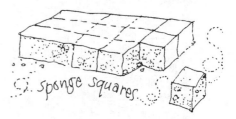
sponge squares

Chocolate Bubble Cakes

Even young children enjoy making rice bubble cakes. For ease of handling later, fill paper cases (in patty pans) with the mixture. OR put a rich caramel filling between two layers of the mixture to make a square for the sweet toothed!

Chocolate Mixture:

1 cup (200g) Kremelta (or Copha), melted
¼ cup cocoa
1 cup icing sugar
4 cups rice bubbles or similar cereal
½ cup chopped dried apricots, sultanas walnuts or coconut, optional

Caramel Filling:

50g butter
2 Tbsp golden syrup
½ of a 400g can sweetened condensed milk
1 tsp vanilla

To make the chocolate mixture, melt the Kremelta (Copha) in a medium sized pot over low heat. When liquid remove from the heat, sift in the cocoa and icing sugar, stir to mix, then add the rice bubbles.

For Bubble Cakes: Stir in two of the optional additions, for extra flavour and texture.

Line 20–30 mini or medium size muffin pans (according to the size of cakes you wish to make) with paper patty tin liners and spoon the mixture into the cases. Leave to set in a cool place.

For Chocolate Bubble Caramel Square: Put all the filling ingredients, except for the vanilla, in the order given, in a medium pot. (Use a household tablespoon to measure the golden syrup, warming it in hot water first.) Bring the mixture to the boil over low heat, stirring constantly and cook for about five minutes or until a little of the mixture dropped in cold water forms a soft ball. Remove from the heat and add the vanilla. Leave to cool slightly.

Line a 20 or 23 cm square cake tin with cling wrap. Pour half the chocolate mixture into it, spread evenly then chill until set. When firm spread with the cooled caramel filling then top with the remaining chocolate mixture. (Reheat over a low heat if the chocolate starts to set before you get to this stage.)

Chill until the chocolate has set before cutting into squares or rectangles with a serrated knife.

Rocky Road

This brightly coloured confection is very popular with children. Make it as an occasional treat — it will certainly brighten a cold, wet day in the holidays. Distribute it in rationed amounts, since it is very rich.

For 30 – 40 squares:

250g cooking chocolate
½ cup (100g) Kremelta (or Copha)
150 – 200g "Eskimos" or marshmallows
100 – 125g jelly-like sweets
1 cup (150g) roasted peanuts

Break up the chocolate and melt with the Kremelta (Copha) in a medium-sized bowl over boiling water, or in a microwave oven until both are liquid. (See instructions for melting chocolate on page 5.) Do not heat more than is necessary or the mixture will be too thin to coat the candy thickly.

Cut the sweets into fairly evenly sized chunks. Cut each "Eskimo" into three pieces and each marshmallow in half. Cut jelly sweets in half. Add with the peanuts to the melted chocolate mixture. Stir to make sure everything is well coated.

Pour into a 23cm square cake tin which has been lined with baking paper or a Teflon liner. Spread the mixture evenly in the tin. Refrigerate until set. (For faster setting, cover and place in the freezer.)

Cut into squares or slices using a knife which has been dipped in hot water.

In warm weather, keep the Rocky Road in a covered container in the refrigerator.

Chocolate Crunchies

As children, we loved the Afghan biscuits my mother made regularly. My streamlined version takes a much shorter time to make and seems just as popular. Sometimes I ice the biscuits, at other times I make them flatter and leave them uniced.

For about 50 biscuits:

125g butter
1 cup sugar
3 Tbsp cocoa
1 tsp vanilla
1 large egg
1 cup self-raising flour
1½ cups malted wheatflakes
50 walnut pieces or halves

In a pot big enough to hold the whole mixture, melt the butter until it is barely liquid, then remove from the heat. Add the sugar, cocoa, vanilla and egg, and mix well with a fork. Measure the flour and wheatflakes on top of this and stir until evenly mixed.

Using two teaspoons, put 50 small, quite compact heaps of mixture on oven trays which have been lightly buttered, sprayed or covered with baking paper or a Teflon liner, leaving room for spreading. The biscuits spread a certain amount as they cook, but if you want larger, flatter biscuits you should flatten the unbaked biscuits gently using several fingers or the pad of your thumb.

Bake at 170°C for 8–12 minutes, until biscuits look evenly cooked but have not darkened round the edges. Transfer to a cooling rack while warm.

When cold, if desired, ice with Sour Cream Biscuit Icing from page 7 and top with walnut pieces or halves before the icing sets. Leave in a cool place for icing to set, then store in an airtight container.

Note: If you are using wheatflakes which have been in your cupboard for some time, spread them on a sponge roll pan and re-crisp them for 3–5 minutes in the oven while it is heating up for the biscuits.

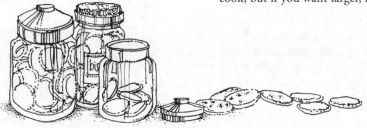

Chocolate Dipped Biscuits

Biscuits dipped in white or brown chocolate make an unusual treat to serve for morning or afternoon coffee, or after a special occasion dinner. Use any shortbread recipe to make the biscuit base. I use a variation of my Custard Kiss recipe.

For about 60 biscuits:

175g butter
¾ cup icing sugar
1 tsp vanilla
1½ cups flour
½ cup custard powder
1 tsp baking powder

Chocolate:

80g dark, milk or white chocolate
2 Tbsp (25g) Kremelta (or Copha)

Put the softened (but not melted) butter in a bowl or food processor. Add the icing sugar and vanilla, then stir in the sifted flour, custard powder and baking powder. Knead the dough on a lightly floured board until smooth. Wrap in plastic film and refrigerate until firm enough to roll out.

On a lightly floured surface roll out the dough to 5mm thickness. Cut heart, star or other shapes from the dough using biscuit cutters. Re-roll the scraps of dough to make more biscuits.

Lifting the biscuits carefully so as not to distort their shape, place the cut shapes on oven trays that have been lightly buttered or sprayed or lined with a Teflon liner.

Bake at 160–170°C for 9–10 minutes, until they feel firm but have not browned at all. Use the lower temperature if the biscuits have been rolled very thinly, or if they are of uneven thickness. They need careful watching, as they brown very quickly once they start. Cool on a rack.

Melt the chocolate and Kremelta (Copha) together, (see instructions on page 58). Dip cold biscuits into warm chocolate to half cover each one. Place carefully on a rack to set. Store in an airtight container.

See photograph on page 23.

Chocolate Cookies

Over the years I have simplified the way I make these three favourites — now I can make them even more quickly than they get eaten.

Kiwi Biscuits

A good old New Zealand favourite!

For 30–50 biscuits:

125g butter
½ cup sugar
3 Tbsp sweetened condensed milk
1 tsp vanilla
1 large egg
1½ cups flour
1 tsp baking powder
½ cup chocolate chips or 100g dark chocolate, chopped

Melt the butter in a medium-sized container until just liquid. Remove from the heat, add the sugar, condensed milk, vanilla and egg, then beat with a fork to mix.

Sift together the flour and baking powder and add with the chocolate to the butter mixture. Stir until well combined.

Roll teaspoonfuls of the mixture into balls and place on oven trays which have been lightly buttered or sprayed with non-stick spray, or lined with baking paper or a Teflon liner. Press each ball with the back of a fork to flatten.

Bake at 180°C for 15–20 minutes, or until very lightly coloured. Lift onto a wire rack to cool.

When cold, store in an airtight container.

Orange Chippies

Great for lunch boxes or with a glass of milk after school.

For 20–30 biscuits:

75g butter
½ cup white sugar
½ cup brown sugar
grated rind of 1 orange
1 large egg
1 cup flour
½ tsp baking soda
½ cup chocolate chips or 100g dark chocolate, chopped

Melt the butter in a medium-sized container until just liquid. Remove from the heat, add the sugars, grated orange rind and egg and beat with a fork.

Chocolate Cookies

I like these biscuits made so they spread out quite a long way and are not thicker in the middle. If you want firmer, more compact biscuits add one or two extra tablespoons of flour.

Sift the flour and baking soda and add with the chocolate to the butter mixture. Stir until well combined.

Place teaspoonfuls on oven trays which have been lightly buttered, sprayed with non-stick spray or lined with baking paper or a Teflon liner. Leave room for the biscuits to spread.

Bake at 180°C for 8–10 minutes or until golden brown. Transfer to a cooling rack.

When cold, store in an airtight container.

Variation: For plain "Chippies" leave out the orange rind.

Peanut Brownies

Peanut Brownies never lose their popularity.

For 30–50 biscuits:

125g butter
1 cup sugar
1 large egg
1 cup flour
2 tsp baking powder
2 Tbsp cocoa
1½ cups lightly roasted peanuts

Melt the butter in a medium-sized pot over low heat until liquid but not hot. Remove from the heat, add the sugar and the egg and stir to combine. Add the sifted dry ingredients and peanuts and stir until well combined.

Roll into balls about the size of a walnut or, using two teaspoons, put spoonfuls of the mixture on a lightly sprayed or Teflon lined oven tray, leaving room for the biscuits to spread.

Bake at 190°C for 10–12 minutes. Do not let biscuits darken around the edges. Leave to stand for about 5 minutes before lifting onto a wire rack. When cold, store in an airtight container.

Note: To lightly roast peanuts for this recipe, bake at 150°C for 15 minutes. Cool before using.

Chocolate Surprise Muffins

You may choose to make these muffins with or without the surprise!
We like them most of all with raspberry jam but they are very good without it too.

Makes 12 medium muffins:

1¾ cups flour
4 tsp baking powder
¼ cup cocoa
½ cup sugar
½ cup (100g) chocolate chips
75g butter, melted
2 large eggs
¾ cup milk

¾ – 1 cup raspberry jam
extra chocolate chips

Sift the flour, baking powder and cocoa into a medium-sized bowl. Add the sugar and chocolate chips and toss with a fork to mix.

Heat the butter in the microwave, or in a pot over low heat on the stove until just liquid. Remove from the heat and add the eggs and milk and beat with a fork until well combined and smooth.

Pour the liquids into the dry ingredients and fold together, mixing as little as possible. Stop as soon as there are no pockets of flour left. For tender muffins with rounded tops, the mixture should be rough and lumpy! Overmixing spoils muffins.

Muffins can stick like crazy! Even though you may have non-stick pans, as an extra precaution, coat them lightly with non-stick spray.

Half fill each muffin pan by spooning about a tablespoon of the mixture into the prepared tins, helping the mixture off with another spoon rather than letting it drop off by itself.

Using a damp teaspoon make a small hollow in each muffin and fill it with a teaspoon of the jam. Divide the remaining mixture between the muffins ensuring that the jam is completely covered.

Sprinkle the muffins with extra chocolate chips and bake at 200°C for about 10 minutes or until the centres spring back when pressed. Leave to stand in the pan for several minutes, until when pressed down gently around the edges and twisted, they will turn freely.

Lift out and leave to cool on a rack.

Chocolate Shortcake

When we were young my mother cooked two or three course dinners every day! She had a large repertoire of puddings, and this chocolate flavoured shortcake was one of our favourites. It is a good choice for guests since it reheats well.

For about 8 servings:

125g cold butter
½ cup self-raising flour
1 cup plain flour
¼ cup cocoa
½ cup sugar
1 large egg
1–2 Tbsp milk
2–3 cups well drained stewed apple or 567g can apple slices, well drained or about ½ cup raspberry or blackcurrant jam

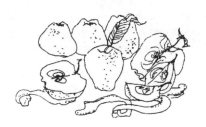

Cut the butter into nine small cubes and process with the flours, cocoa and sugar until finely chopped. Add the egg and mix again, then add enough milk to make a mixture firm enough to press into a pan like a crumb crust.

Without a food processor grate the chilled butter into the dry ingredients in a bowl, gradually add the egg that has been lightly beaten with a fork, then add enough milk to form a crumbly dough.

Prepare a 23cm (preferably loose-bottomed) round or square tin by lining its bottom with baking paper or a non-stick liner. Spray or butter the exposed sides of the tin.

Press half the crumbly mixture into the bottom of the prepared tin, then spread with the drained apples or jam then crumble the remaining dough over the filling. Press it down lightly to form an even layer.

Bake at 170–180°C for about 30–45 minutes, until the dough in the middle feels firm. A shortcake cooked in a round tin is likely to need the longer cooking time. Leave to cool slightly before removing from the tin.

Sprinkle with icing sugar and serve warm, with lightly whipped cream or vanilla icecream.

Variation: Beat the softened butter with the sugar for a smoother textured shortcake, if you do not mind the extra work.

Chocolate Bread Pudding

This is not your ordinary old bread and butter pudding! I hope you will try it for a treat. Children love the meringue topped variation.

For 4–6 servings:

about 75g stale French bread, bread rolls or currant bread
1 cup milk
½ cup cream
½ cup chocolate chips or 100g dark chocolate, chopped
¼ cup sugar
2 large eggs
2 Tbsp rum, optional

Butter a baking dish about 20 x 16cm. Cut bread into small slices about 1cm thick. Arrange overlapping slices attractively in the dish, filling it evenly.

Heat the milk, cream, chocolate chips or broken chocolate and sugar in a pot over moderate heat, stirring constantly until the chocolate has dissolved.

Beat the eggs until well mixed but not frothy, add the rum, then pour the hot chocolate mixture into the egg mixture through a fine sieve. Mix well, then pour over the bread in the baking dish.

Leave to stand for at least 15 minutes before baking, spooning the liquid over the bread at intervals to make sure there are no unsoaked pieces.

Stand baking dish in a roasting pan containing enough hot water to come at least half way up the sides of the dish. Bake uncovered at 180°C for 30–40 minutes, until the centre feels set and a sharp knife pushed into the middle comes out clean.

Serve warm, dusted with icing sugar.

Variation: Use three eggs instead of two. Separate the whites and the yolks. Use the yolks with the milk etc. to make the custard and beat the whites with an extra ¼ cup of sugar to make meringue. Brush raspberry jam thinly over the cooked custard, spread the meringue attractively over the top and return to the oven until the meringue is lightly browned and crisp. Serve warm, not hot.

Chocolate Upside Down Cake

There are times when spectacular family puddings are called for, even though they often have to be prepared and cooked in a short time! This quick, easy pudding looks as if you have spent hours slaving over a hot stove.

For 6–8 servings:

Topping:

425g can peaches or pears
1 Tbsp butter, melted
1 tsp custard powder
1 Tbsp juice from can
2 Tbsp golden syrup
chopped walnuts or cherries, optional

Cake:

50g butter
½ cup brown sugar
1 large egg
1 cup flour
2 Tbsp cocoa
½ tsp baking soda
juice from can, to mix

Put the fruit in a sieve to drain, saving all the juice.

Melt the butter for the topping in a lightly sprayed microwave ring pan. Stir in the custard powder, juice and golden syrup. Microwave on High for about 45 seconds, or until mixture boils and thickens slightly. Sprinkle the walnuts or cherries in the ring pan, then arrange the drained fruit attractively around the dish.

To make the cake soften the butter, beat with the sugar and egg using a rotary beater, fork, or food processor. Sift the dry ingredients over this, add about 2 tablespoons of the reserved juice, and mix everything together. As you mix, add extra liquid, using as much as you need to make a batter soft enough to drop from a spoon.

Drop this in spoonfuls evenly over the fruit. Do not worry if there are unfilled areas, as the cake mixture spreads as it cooks. Cover the microwave dish with a lid, or for faster, more even rising, with vented plastic film.

Place the dish in the microwave oven on a rack, or on an upturned plate, and cook on Medium-High (70%) power for 10—12 minutes, or until the mixture close to the central cone is cooked. If in doubt, cook a little longer. Leave cake to stand for 2-3 minutes, then turn out on a flat plate and lift away the ring pan.

Serve warm, plain or with icecream.

Chocolate Fudge Pudding

I have yet to meet the child who doesn't like this self-saucing pudding. Here is the simplest version I can think of. You won't be left with a kitchen full of dirty dishes, whatever the age of the cook!

For 4 servings:

25g butter
1 cup self-raising flour
2 Tbsp cocoa
½ cup white sugar
½ cup milk
1 tsp vanilla

Topping:

2 Tbsp cocoa
½ cup brown sugar
¼ – ½ cup chopped walnuts, optional
1 Tbsp butter
1¾ cups boiling water

Spray a 20cm round, fairly deep baking dish with non-stick spray. Melt the butter in this dish then add the next 5 ingredients in the order given, without stirring. Mix with a fork to make a fairly stiff dough. Spread it evenly over the bottom of the dish.

To make the topping, sprinkle over this, as evenly as you can, the cocoa, brown sugar and the nuts, if used. Dot the butter evenly over this.

Pour the boiling water carefully over everything, wetting the whole surface.

To cook conventionally: Bake uncovered at 180°C for 20–30 minutes, until the top feels quite firm and springy in the middle. Check the centre with a small pointed knife to make sure the cakey part just under the crust in the middle is cooked.

To microwave: Mix batter in a separate bowl, and spread evenly in a sprayed or lightly buttered microwave ring pan. Prepare topping as above. Cover with a paper towel and cook on Medium-High (70%) power for about 10 minutes, or until the whole surface feels springy. Serve from the ring pan or invert onto a flat plate if you like. Serve hot or warm with icecream. If cooked for the correct time, the pudding should have a nicely thickened sauce under it.

Variation: Add a sliced or mashed banana, a grated apple or chopped walnuts to the dry ingredients.

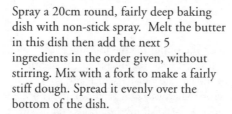

Chocolate Custard

This very simple pudding can be made in just a few minutes. It is easy for children to make themselves. Try the variations and see which version is most popular in your household.

For 4 servings:

½ cup (100g) chocolate chips
¼ cup sugar
¼ cup cornflour or custard powder
2 cups milk

To microwave: Measure the chocolate chips, sugar and cornflour or custard powder into a microwave bowl or jug, mix together thoroughly then add the milk and stir again until all ingredients are well combined.

Cook for 3 minutes on High, take the container out and stir with a whisk. Don't worry if it doesn't look chocolatey at this stage. Return to the microwave and cook for a further 3 minutes, or until it starts to bubble on top. Stir with a whisk again, until the mixture is very smooth.

The mixture gets smoother, thicker and darker as the chocolate melts through it.

To cook conventionally: Measure the chocolate chips, sugar and cornflour or custard powder into a medium-sized pot. Mix well, then add the milk and stir to mix all the ingredients. Bring to the boil, stirring all the time, and keep stirring and heating until the pudding is dark and smooth.

To serve, pour into individual dishes, allow to cool and top with whipped cream, chopped roasted nuts, fresh berries or sliced fruit. Refrigerate until required.

Variations:

- For Peanutty Custard: Add ¼ cup peanut butter before heating.
- For Cheesecake Custard: Replace ¼ cup of milk with ¼ cup of cream cheese.
- For Banana Custard: Add 1–2 sliced bananas as the pudding cools.

Chocolate Pear Custard

Pears and chocolate seem to be made to go together! This easy pudding is very popular with children.

For 4–6 servings:
2 Tbsp custard powder
3 Tbsp cocoa
3 Tbsp sugar
1 large egg
1½ cups milk
425g can pears
1 Tbsp butter
½ tsp vanilla

Mix the custard powder, cocoa and sugar together in a medium-sized pot, so you will not get a lumpy mixture later. Add the egg, mix well then stir in the milk and the juice drained from the can of pears.

Bring to the boil, stirring all the time. As soon as the mixture is hot, add the butter and vanilla and keep stirring and heating until the pudding is dark, thick and bubbling round the edges.

Remove from the heat and, while the pudding cools, chop the pears into smaller pieces. Put in four to six individual dishes and pour the custard on top, or put the custard into the dishes and put the pears on top.

Serve plain or top with a little runny cream or whipped cream and decorate with chopped nuts.

Variation: For a party pudding, let the custard cool completely, then layer it in glasses, with the chopped drained pears and whipped cream.

Chocolate Pear Custard

Chocolate Mousse

Chocolate Mousse

This chocolate mousse is an exceedingly rich mixture which should be served in very small amounts only on special occasions. Having given you this warning, I must add that it is also very good and exceedingly popular with "chocoholics".

For 8–12 servings:

500g dark chocolate
½ cup hot water
2 tsp instant coffee
juice & finely grated rind of 2 oranges
3 large eggs, separated

Break the chocolate into even sized squares. Heat it with the water, instant coffee, orange juice and very finely grated orange rind in the microwave, on Defrost (30%) power, for 6–7 minutes or until the chocolate has melted. Stir until the mixture is smooth. If you do not have a microwave, heat everything in a bowl over hot (but preferably not boiling) water until the chocolate has melted. Stir until smooth.

Remove from the heat. Add the egg yolks and beat well.

Beat egg whites until stiff and fold carefully into the chocolate mixture.

Pour the mixture into 8–12 small glasses and refrigerate for at least 2 hours before serving. Garnish as desired with lightly whipped cream and chocolate curls (see page 59).

The mixture may be made up to 2 days before it is needed, but it will be considerably firmer (but still very good) after this time.

If you are working well ahead, consider pouring the mixture into a lined loaf tin and refrigerating for at least 24 hours or up to 4 days. Unmould, and cut in slices. Serve with fresh grapes and/or biscotti for contrasting colours, flavour and texture.

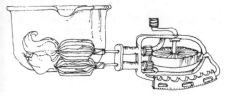

Chocolate Icecream

This easy-to-make icecream does not require a second beating, and keeps well in a covered container in the freezer for several weeks without going hard and icy.

For 1 litre:

2 large eggs, separated
½ cup caster sugar
2 Tbsp cocoa
¼ cup boiling water
½ tsp vanilla
1 cup cream

Separate the eggs. Put the whites in a medium - large bowl and the yolks in a separate bowl. Beat the whites until soft peaks form, add half the sugar and beat until the mixture forms peaks which turn over at the top when the beater is lifted out.

In a small container, mix the cocoa and boiling water, stirring to dissolve any lumps. Add the cocoa mixture to the egg yolks, with the remaining sugar and vanilla. Beat until the mixture is very thick and fluffy, nearly as stiff as the egg white mixture. Pour over the beaten egg whites. Scrape the bowl well, then measure in the cream.

Beat the cream until quite thick, but soft enough to drop from a spoon or beater. Pour cream over the two egg mixtures and fold gently to combine the three. Don't worry about mixing until the chocolate is completely combined, since the icecream looks very nice when served, with streaks of white through it.

Pour the mixture into a suitable container which will hold at least 1 litre. Cover and freeze immediately.

Variations: Replace vanilla with almond or peppermint essence. Add toasted, chopped nuts such as almonds, walnuts or hazelnuts. Stir through the mixture just before freezing.

Note: This recipe contains uncooked egg whites and yolks, for this reason it should not be given to very young children.

Chocolate Velvet Pudding

*I have made this pudding since my children were preschoolers.
My little granddaughters enjoy it just as much as their mother did!*

For 8 servings:

400g can chilled unsweetened condensed milk (evaporated milk)
2 Tbsp gelatine
½ cup milk
6 (level) Tbsp cocoa
1 cup sugar
½ cup water
½ tsp vanilla

The unsweetened condensed milk must be very cold if it is to beat up to a good volume. Put it in the refrigerator 24 hours ahead; or freeze it in a bowl until it is cold enough to form ice crystals; or if you are really short of time chill it quickly in a larger container covering it with cold water containing lots of iceblocks.

Measure the gelatine into a small bowl. Mix with the milk and leave to soften while you mix the cocoa and sugar in a pot. Add the water, and bring to the boil, stirring all the time. Remove from the heat and stir in the softened gelatine and the vanilla. Stand the pot in cold water to cool this mixture until it is thick but not set. (If it sets, warm it until it liquefies again.)

Beat the chilled milk in a large bowl until very thick and frothy. Slowly pour in the cold (but still liquid) gelatine mixture, beating all the time.

As soon as the two mixtures have been blended, pour into two bowls, or into about 8 individual bowls to set. Cover and refrigerate for up to two days. (The pudding will darken as it stands.)

Serve with canned peaches and lightly whipped cream, or top with whipped cream and chopped nuts.

Hazelnut Chocolate Pie

This delicious pie tastes wonderful made with hazelnuts, but you may like to ring in the changes, using chopped walnuts, pecans or a mixture of several different nuts (including pinenuts).

For 8 - 12 servings:

Pastry:

1¼ cups flour
75g butter
3–4 Tbsp cold water
2 tsp lemon juice

Filling:

100g dark chocolate
100g cold butter
½ cup brown sugar
¼ cup golden syrup
3 large eggs
1 cup (125g) hazelnuts, lightly roasted
1 tsp vanilla

To make the pastry, measure the flour into a food processor bowl. Add the butter, cut into 9 cubes. Do not process.

Acidify the water with the lemon juice (to make the pastry tender). Using the pulse button, add the water in a thin stream while chopping the butter through the flour. Test at intervals to see if the dough particles are moist enough to press together with your fingers to form a ball. The mixture will look crumbly at this stage. (If a ball of dough forms in the processor, you have added too much water.)

Chill pastry for 5–10 minutes before rolling out on a lightly floured surface. Gently ease pastry into 23cm flan dish and trim the edges.

To make the filling, break the chocolate into even pieces then heat with the butter, brown sugar and golden syrup until the sugar has dissolved and the chocolate has melted. Leave to cool. Beat in the eggs until blended.

Chop the nuts roughly, using a sharp knife rather than a food processor, then stir into the chocolate mixture with the vanilla.

Pour the filling into the prepared pastry base and bake at 170°C for 20–30 minutes, or until the top feels slightly firm. If the mixture rises up during cooking, deflate with a skewer or sharp knife.

Leave to cool for 15 minutes before removing from the tin. Serve at room temperature. Dust lightly with icing sugar before serving with icecream or whipped cream.

Almond & Rum Fudge Tart

This rich tart is ideal for a special occasion dessert. It does require a little time and effort, but your friends and family should be thrilled and impressed when you serve it. When cut, a dark, delicious, soft centre is revealed.

For 8 –10 servings:

Base:
1 packet (250g) Digestive biscuits
100g butter

Filling:
3 large eggs
1 cup sugar
3 Tbsp cocoa
1 cup (120g) ground almonds
½ cup cream
2 Tbsp rum

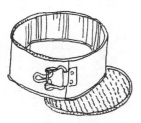

To make the base crumb the biscuits, using a food processor if available, or put them into a plastic bag and crush with a rolling pin.

Melt the butter and add biscuit crumbs. Mix well and press the mixture onto the bottom and about 4cm up the sides of a 23cm springform or loose bottomed cake tin using the back of a spoon. Refrigerate while you make the filling.

To make the filling, use a food processor or electric beater to beat the eggs and sugar together until thick and fluffy. Add the cocoa, ground almonds, cream and rum, and mix briefly to combine.

Pour the filling into the prepared base and bake at 180°C for 25–30 minutes until the top and edges of the cake feel firm, but the centre is still soft. The cake will firm up as it cools, but should be very soft in the centre. Leave to stand overnight, or for several hours. When the cake has cooled, trim the edges of the crust with a sharp knife if necessary, and carefully remove from the tin.

Serve at room temperature with lightly whipped cream and sprinkled with toasted slivered almonds.

Note: For easiest slicing use a hot wet knife.

Variations: Replace rum with orange juice or very strong coffee if desired.

Sumptuous Sauces

One of the easiest and most popular desserts you can make is icecream with chocolate sauce. Here are five interesting sauces to try. Leftovers keep for several days if chilled, but may thicken as they stand. Reheat if necessary.

Chocolate Sorcery

Dress up icecream and chocolate sauce.

Serve with fruit such as: bananas, peaches, pears, apricots, strawberries, raspberries, blackberries, kiwifruit, grapes, melons, fresh cherries etc.

Top sauce with: chopped nuts, toasted coconut, coconut threads, hundreds and thousands, chopped candy, jelly crystals, chocolate chips, maraschino cherries, chopped dried fruit, toasted seeds etc.

Push one or more sweets into the side of your homemade sundae to please young children. Use: pink wafers, flaked chocolate bars, jelly beans, jelly aeroplanes, snakes, dinosaurs etc., marshmallows, pineapple lumps, chocolate fish etc.

Chocolate Peanut Sauce

For 1 cup:

¾ cup chocolate chips or 150g chocolate, chopped
¼ cup peanut butter
¼ cup milk

Measure all ingredients into a small microwave jug. Heat on Medium (50%) power for 2 minutes. Stir until smooth.

To cook conventionally, heat ingredients in a small pot over a low heat, stirring constantly until mixture is smooth and thick.

Thin with extra milk if necessary. The mixture will thicken on cooling. Reheat before use, adding more milk if it is too thick.

Top with chopped roasted peanuts if desired.

Chocolate Coconut Sauce

For 1 cup:

½ cup chocolate chips or 100g chocolate, chopped
½ cup coconut milk

Measure ingredients into a small microwave jug. Heat on Medium (50%) power for 2 minutes. Stir until smooth.

To cook conventionally, heat in a small pot over a low heat, stirring constantly until mixture is smooth. Do not boil.

Reheat before serving.

Top with toasted coconut threads if desired.

Sumptuous Sauces

To delight your children, keep your favourite chocolate sauce in a squeeze bottle in the fridge. Warm if necessary, then squeeze it out to write words or draw pictures on a plate. Scoop icecream on top and decorate with fruit to make faces etc.

Creamy Chocolate Sauce

For ¾ cup:

½ cup chocolate chips or 100g chocolate, chopped
½ cup cream or sour cream

Measure ingredients into a small microwave jug. Heat on Medium (50%) power for 2 minutes. Stir until smooth.

To cook conventionally, heat in a small pot over a low heat, stirring constantly until smooth. Do not allow to boil.

Reheat before serving.

Chocolate Fudge Sauce

For ¾ cup:

¼ cup cocoa
1 cup brown sugar
50g butter
½ cup milk
½ tsp vanilla

Measure cocoa and sugar into a small pot. Mix well until there are no lumps.

Add cubed butter, milk and vanilla. Bring to the boil over low heat, stirring constantly until the sugar has dissolved. Boil for two minutes, then remove from the heat.

Serve immediately, or reheat in a microwave or in a pot over a low heat.

Chocolate Velvet Sauce

For 1¼ cups:

½ cup chocolate chips or 100g chocolate, chopped
½ cup sweetened condensed milk
½ cup cream

Measure ingredients into a small microwave jug. Heat on Medium (50%) power for 2 minutes. Stir until smooth.

To cook conventionally, heat in a small pot over a low heat, stirring constantly until smooth. Do not allow to boil.

Reheat before serving.

Chocolate Fondue

People of all ages seem to enjoy sitting around a communal pot of Chocolate Fondue dipping into it. You may be surprised how quickly the fruit disappears! Be realistic – provide protection for clothes and furniture, or serve your fondue outside!

200 - 250g dark, milk or cooking chocolate, or chocolate chips
½ cup cream
grated rind of 1 orange or 1–2 Tbsp brandy, rum or liqueur

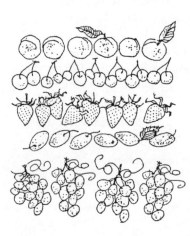

Break the chocolate into squares or small pieces, and place in a flat-bottomed microwave dish. Pour the cream over the chocolate, then very finely grate all the coloured rind from the orange into the mixture.

Microwave on High for 2 minutes, leave to stand for 1 minute, then stir until the chocolate and cream are evenly mixed. If there are any remaining lumps, microwave again in 20 second bursts, until lumps disappear when stirred. If adding spirits, stir into the cooked mixture.

Pour the warm mixture in to the serving dish, or put aside for later reheating and serving.

Pile generous amounts of bite-sized pieces of fruit on a flat plate around the hot chocolate dip. (Prepare the fruit ahead and refrigerate in plastic bags until required, if desired.)

Suitable fruits include:

apricots	oranges
apples	nashi
bananas	paw-paw
cherries	peaches
grapes	pears
kiwifruit	pineapple
melons	strawberries

Chocolate Fondue

Brandy Truffles (see page 54), Chocolate Fudge, Homemade Chocolates (see page 57), Chocolate Dipped Apricots (see page 58)

Melt-in-the-Mouth Chocolate Fudge

If you can master the finer points of making wonderful creamy fudge, your reputation as a good sweet maker will be assured! Good fudge must be cooked just enough, beaten carefully, and turned out just before it starts to set.

For 64 squares:

3 cups sugar
¼ cup cocoa
¼ tsp cream of tartar
1 cup milk
50g butter
1 tsp vanilla

Stir together in a pot of about 23cm diameter the sugar, cocoa and cream of tartar until no lumps remain. Add the milk and the butter cut in four cubes, then cook over low to moderate heat, stirring all the time, until the sugar melts. By this stage there must be no grains of sugar on the sides of the pot. Use a flexible spatula to remove them or put on the lid for one to two minutes.

Raise heat until mixture is bubbling vigorously all over the surface, but is not climbing too high up the sides of the pot! After 5 minutes start dropping half teaspoon lots into a bowl containing cold water at least 5 cm deep. The fudge is ready when the mixture on the bottom of the water container can be pushed into a soft ball which keeps its shape when lifted out of the water (probably after 8–10 minutes).

Cool pot until you can hold your hand against the bottom, then beat constantly with a spatula until you can see the fudge starting to set around the edges. Quickly pour into a buttered (20 cm square) container before it sets. Swirl top, then leave to finish setting. Cut into 8 squares each way.

Notes: If you are new to fudge-making, make half quantities, reducing the boiling time to about 5 minutes, until you "get the feel" of the mixture. Hard fudge has cooked too long but will still be enjoyed! Fudge which does not set may be warmed with a little sour or fresh cream to make fudge sauce for icecream. Chocolate fudge is more difficult to make than other fudges which do not contain cocoa. Practice makes perfect, however!

Tempting Truffles

Truffles make wonderful gifts whether you put a few in a cellophane bag tied with curling ribbon, arrange a selection in gift boxes, or present one or more varieties in a pretty lidded jar.

Jaffa Truffles

1 cup currants
2 tsp very finely grated orange rind
¼ cup rum, brandy or orange juice
250g (2½ cups) chocolate cake crumbs
100g (½ cup) chocolate chips, melted

Plump up the currants by pouring boiling water over them in a sieve. Dry on paper towels then put in a bowl with the very finely grated orange rind, and the spirit of your choice or orange juice.

Crumb the cakes using a food processor, or by hand. Add the crumbs and the melted chocolate to the currant mixture.

Mix well together, then roll into small walnut-sized balls. The balls can be rolled in coconut, cocoa or icing sugar.

Store in the refrigerator or freezer.

Brandy Balls

250g packet plain (sweet) biscuits
225g butter, softened
½ cup cocoa
1½ cups icing sugar
¼ cup sweetened condensed milk
3 Tbsp brandy
½ cup sultanas, chopped
¼ cup walnuts, finely chopped
coconut for rolling

Crumb biscuits finely using a food processor or rolling pin.

Mix butter, cocoa and icing sugar then beat in condensed milk, brandy, chopped sultanas, walnuts and biscuit crumbs.

Chill if necessary, then roll in small balls and coat with coconut.

Variation: Replace brandy with sherry, rum, strong coffee or orange juice.

Mocha Truffles

100g butter
2 cups icing sugar
¼ cup cocoa
½ cup chopped sultanas
¾ cup coconut
1 tsp instant coffee
1 Tbsp sherry or rum
extra coconut for rolling

Mix the softened butter with the sifted icing sugar and cocoa.

Chop sultanas, with a wet knife. Add to butter mixture with the coconut and coffee dissolved in the sherry or rum.

For easier handling, chill mixture if necessary. Form into small balls with a teaspoon, and roll in more coconut.

Refrigerate or freeze.

Tempting Truffles

When making truffles you may find your mixture is too dry or too wet. Add extra liquid to moisten the mixture or extra crumbs or coconut to firm it up. If coconut coatings will not stick, dampen surface with a little sherry or fruit juice first.

White Chocolate Truffles

200–250g sponge cake
½ cup red glace cherries, roughly chopped
2 Tbsp Kirsch
100g white chocolate, melted

Crumb the cake using a food processor, or by hand. In a medium-sized bowl mix together the cake crumbs, glace cherries and Kirsch. Add the melted chocolate and mix.

Roll into small balls.

The balls can be rolled in coconut while still moist, then stored in the refrigerator, or chilled then rolled in icing sugar just before serving, or chilled then dipped in white chocolate.

Variation: Replace Kirsch with sherry and add a little almond essence.

Tipplers' Treat

50g butter
1 Tbsp golden syrup
¼ cup whisky, brandy, rum or sherry
¾ cup icing sugar
1 Tbsp cocoa
200g plain (sweet) biscuits, crumbed
icing sugar to dust

Melt the butter, add a rounded household tablespoon of golden syrup and the spirits of your choice, or sherry. Stir in the sifted icing sugar and cocoa, add the finely crumbed biscuits and stir to combine. If final mixture seems dry, add a little extra melted butter. If it is too moist, add more crumbs, or coconut, or chill the mixture.

Roll into small balls and chill until firm. Dust with icing sugar just before serving.

Refrigerate or freeze.

Liqueur Truffles

150g dark chocolate
2 Tbsp orange liqueur, or brandy
2 Tbsp butter
1 egg yolk
¼ cup cocoa

Break the chocolate up if necessary. Put into a suitable container with the alcohol of your choice and heat, in a microwave on Defrost (30%) power for 3–4 minutes, or in a basin over boiling water until the chocolate has softened and can be mixed smoothly with the liqueur.

Add the butter and egg yolk and mix until well combined. (The warm chocolate will melt the butter.) Leave for 3–4 hours at room temperature before rolling into walnut sized balls. Roll each ball in cocoa.

Store in the refrigerator or freezer.

Homemade Chocolates

Don't be intimidated by the idea of making chocolates yourself. If you work your way quietly through the various steps until you are familiar with the techniques you will find that you can produce spectacular results.

Steps in chocolate making

1. Prepare the filling.
2. Leave the filling to set in the pot for several hours or overnight.
3. Flavour the fillings (optional) and shape into small balls etc.
4. Chill the balls until they are very cold and firm.
5. Dip the chilled fillings into chocolate coating.
6. Chill the completed chocolates until they are to be eaten.

If you try to rush from one step to the next without allowing chilling time you will find your task is much harder.

Sinfully Rich Chocolates

This recipe makes the most delicious chocolates with a smooth, rich, melt-in-the-mouth filling.

For 40–50 chocolates:

Basic Filling:

½ cup cream
200g dark chocolate
50g butter
½ cup coconut cream

Coating:

200g dark chocolate or chocolate chips
2 Tbsp (25g) Kremelta (or Copha)

Heat the cream in a pot until it is hot but not boiling. Remove from the heat, add the chocolate, broken into small pieces and the butter, in 6 - 8 small cubes.

Leave in a warm place for 5 minutes then stir well. If the chocolate has not melted, warm the pot in a bowl of hot water. When mixture is smooth, stir in the coconut cream. Chill overnight or for several hours, until firm.

The mixture makes a good filling as it is. If you like you can divide it into several parts and flavour each using essences such as rum essence, almond essence, peppermint essence, Kirsch essence or fruit flavoured essences.

When you use a fruit flavoured essence you should mix it with a few crystals of citric acid first. Make sure the citric acid is dissolved before you use it. I find the easiest way to flavour the filling is to put the flavouring, citric acid if used, and filling on a sheet of plastic (plastic bag) and fold the plastic over the mixture so you can knead everything through the plastic.

Shape the filling into small balls. To keep everything cold, handle mixture as little as possible. Cover and chill or freeze, taking care not to get any ice crystals on the fillings.

Homemade Chocolates

Present your homemade chocolates really attractively for maximum effect. Look in stationers, gift shops and specialty food shops for small paper or foil cases, shallow lidded boxes and suitable ribbons, wraps and gift tags.

To make the coating melt 1 tablespoon of Kremelta (Copha) in a small bowl over hot but not boiling water, then add the chocolate, broken into small pieces. Stir until smooth and creamy, adding as little Kremelta (Copha) as you need to make a chocolate of good coating consistency. (If you add too much, the chocolate coating is too thin.) Drop the chilled or frozen balls of filling into the chocolate one at a time. Lift each one out with a bent fork, or something similar, as soon as it is coated. Slide each onto a sheet of plastic on a tray, then refrigerate until set.

If you find any uncoated sections when you take the set chocolates off the plastic, redip or patch with more chocolate.

Decorate with chocolate squiggle if desired.

Store in the refrigerator, up to a month.

Easy Peppermint Creams

This filling is easy to work with.

25g butter
¼ cup sweetened condensed milk
½ tsp peppermint essence
about 2 cups icing sugar
green food colouring, optional

Have butter soft but not melted. Mix first four ingredients in a bowl or food processor, adding enough icing sugar to form a firm paste. Colour the mixture green, if desired.

Roll in balls. Chill overnight or for several hours. Dip in chocolate (see previous recipe).

Marzipan Chocolates

1 cup (100g) ground almonds
1 cup icing sugar
½ cup caster sugar
1 egg yolk
2 Tbsp strained lemon juice
¼ tsp almond essence, optional
50–60 blanched almonds, optional

Combine the ground almonds and sugars in a mixing bowl or food processor. Mix the egg yolk with half of the lemon juice and add to the almond mixture with a little almond essence if desired.

Add the remaining lemon juice, a little at a time until you have a mixture which is easy to work with. Roll the paste into small balls and chill until firm. Dip in chocolate as described. Top each with a blanched almond if desired.

Chocolate Dipped Delights

Foods dipped in chocolate look so professional (if you have done a good job) that you will really impress your friends and family!

The following pointers should help you get started, but there is nothing like "hands on" experience to teach you. Start by dipping biscuits (page 31) or dried apricots, before you dip strawberries, chocolates, etc.

The coating must be of the correct consistency. If it is too thick it is hard to work with and will be "gluggy". If it is too thin, it will coat the food too lightly, and run off.

You can coat foods with dark, milk, or white chocolate. In many dipping situations you need to thin the chocolate you have melted with a little Kremelta (Copha). This makes it flow better, so it coats the food more smoothly. Don't get carried away, though. If you add too much, you dilute the chocolate flavour and make the coating too thin, and slow down the setting. A dipped chocolate, for example, will finish up standing on a solidified, spread-out puddle of thin fragile chocolate. Add a little at a time, dipping something between additions to check consistency.

The temperature affects the consistency of the dip, too. Melt the dipping mixture over hot water, remove it from the heat when ready, but leave it standing over hot water so that it does not cool down and thicken while you are dipping.

If you melt a little Kremelta (Copha) in your bowl before you add the chocolate, it will melt more easily.

Although you can remelt solidified coating for later use, you do not want to melt a lot more chocolate than you need. A bowl, ramekin or cup may be better than a bowl with a wide base. You want to be able to submerge the food you are dipping.

When you are dipping a chocolate and want a completely smooth surface, stand the uncoated chocolate on a fork with the prongs bent almost to rightangles with the handle, or make yourself a small wire loop, bent the same way.

After dipping, hold the coated food above the chocolate dip so that it can drip, then slip it off its holder onto a piece of plastic. When the chocolate has set, you can peel away the plastic easily.

Chocolate sets faster on chilled food. The chilled food must not be damp, though. Do not dip warm foods since the coating will run off them.

Try dipping biscuits (page 31), Brazil nuts, almonds, dried apricots, dehydrated kiwi-fruit slices, candied peel, truffles, strawberries and chocolates.

Chocolate Decorations

You can make all sorts of interesting shapes with chocolate. Many of these are a matter of trial and error, so you should persevere, experimenting with different kinds of chocolate (see page 5).

Small shavings

Shave lengths of chocolate from the straight edge of a block, using a potato peeler. Notice the way you get different results with chocolate of different temperatures. It must not be too cold, nor too warm for good curls.

Large shavings

Large shavings make impressive cake decorations, as on the cover picture. Melt chocolate (see page 5) then spread it on a clean smooth baking tray and leave it to set. Securing the tray so it does not move, use the edge of a long straight knife, a fish slice or a rectangular bench scraper held at an angle of about 45° to shave off large curls. By moving one end of your scraper faster than the other, you get trumpet-shaped curls. If the chocolate splinters, it is too cold. The temperature of a warm room is about right. Experiment with different chocolate, thicknesses, scrapers and temperatures until you make everything work! When this happens, put the large shavings on non-stick paper to set, and lift them with bamboo skewers since they are very fragile. Dust with icing sugar or leave them as they are.

Shapes

Spread melted chocolate on plastic or baking paper, then cut in shapes with metal biscuit cutters. You can cut the chocolate before it is too hard, or cut firmer chocolate with cutters heated in boiling water. When set, peel off the paper. Experiment with different thicknesses of chocolate, and different shapes.

Moulds

Small purpose-made moulds are easily filled with melted chocolate (see page 5). Level off the tops, refrigerate the moulds, and pop out the chocolates, pushing one edge with the point of a sharp knife if necessary. (I have produced perfectly moulded chocolates with a three year old, in about 15 minutes, using small metal moulds costing about $2 for 8!)

Drawing and writing

Melt chocolate (see page 5) and spoon it into a small unpunctured plastic bag, or try microwaving $1/4$ cup chocolate chips in a small, folded-open plastic bag at 50% power for 2–3 minutes. Secure the top, close to the chocolate, with a rubber band, then snip off the corner of the bag to make a tiny hole. As you squeeze the bag, the melted chocolate is forced out. You can write or draw on a birthday cake; make squiggles or faces on iced cup-cakes; draw pictures, make initials, write names or draw pictures on Teflon liners or plastic which is held flat (with sticky tape) on a working surface. As soon as the chocolate is hard, peel off the plastic.

Chocolate Drinks

Chocolate drinks are certainly not just for children. Have fun trying these drinks at different times of the day, in both hot and cold weather.

Chocolate Syrup

Keep this syrup in the refrigerator to use as the base for different drinks.

½ cup cocoa
½ cup sugar
¾ cup water
1 tsp vanilla

Measure the cocoa and sugar into a medium-sized pot and mix well to make sure there are no lumps.

Add the water and vanilla, stir well and bring to the boil. Boil for 2 minutes and remove from the heat.

When it has cooled the syrup can be kept refrigerated for up to one week.

Hot Chocolate

Just as suitable last thing at night as it is early in the morning!

For 1 serving:
2 Tbsp Chocolate Syrup
1 cup milk

Mix the Chocolate Syrup and milk together in a microwaveable mug or a small pot. Heat until nearly boiling.

Serve at once. For special occasions, top with marshmallows or whipped cream.

Hot Mocha

Quick easy and a little different — popular with teenagers and adults.

For 1 serving:
1 Tbsp Chocolate Syrup
1 tsp instant coffee
1 cup milk

Mix the Chocolate Syrup and instant coffee together until the coffee has dissolved. Add the milk, stir well and heat in a microwaveable mug or a small pot until the mixture is nearly boiling.

Serve with whipped cream, and a little grated chocolate sprinkled on top.

Chocolate Egg Nog

A meal in a glass – just the thing for anyone who needs cheering up!

For 2 servings:
3 Tbsp Chocolate Syrup
1½ cups milk
1 egg, separated
few grains salt
1 Tbsp sugar
1–2 Tbsp rum, optional

Beat together the Chocolate Syrup, milk and egg yolk. Heat until the mixture bubbles round the edges and thickens slightly.

Chocolate Drinks

For maximum impact, serve your drinks as attractively as possible, using interesting mugs and glasses, long spoons, straws and garnishes etc.

In a clean bowl, beat the egg whites with a few grains of salt until foamy. Add the sugar and beat until peaks turn over.

Strain the hot chocolate mixture into the beaten egg white and whisk again until the whole mixture is evenly coloured. Stir in the rum if using it.

Hot Rich Chocolate

For a wonderful start to the weekend, try this with a croissant!

For 1 serving:

40–50g dark chocolate or 3–4 Tbsp
    chocolate chips
2 Tbsp water
1 cup milk

Break up the chocolate if necessary. Heat the chocolate and water together in a microwaveable mug or a small pot, until the chocolate has melted. Stir until smooth. Add the milk and heat again until nearly boiling. Stir until well combined. If using a pot, pour the hot drink into a mug.

Top with marshmallows or a spoonful of whipped cream or sprinkle a little grated chocolate over the top.

Iced Mocha

A cooling, nutritious drink for a hot day.

For 1 serving:

1 tsp instant coffee
1 Tbsp hot water
1 Tbsp Chocolate Syrup
1 cup milk, chilled
4–6 iceblocks

Stir instant coffee and the hot water together in a medium-sized jug. Add the Chocolate Syrup and chilled milk and stir or whisk until combined.

Pour over iceblocks into a tall glass and serve with a straw.

Chocolate Spider

You may find that adults enjoy this as well as children.

Chocolate Icecream (see page 44)
Coca Cola, chilled

Measure a scoop of Chocolate Icecream into a tall glass. Pour chilled Coca Cola over and whisk with a fork until the mixture is fluffy.

Serve with a long straw.

Variation: For Jaffa Spider, pour chilled orange flavoured fizzy drink over the icecream.

Index

Almond & rum fudge tart	47	Chocolate banana cake	15	Chocolate sponge, three minute	16
Applecake, chocolate	10	Chocolate bread pudding	36	Chocolate surprise muffins	34
Aunt Lucy's mistake	19	Chocolate bubble cakes	28	Chocolate syrup	60
Balls, brandy	54	Chocolate caramel bars	26	Chocolate upside down cake	37
Banana cake, chocolate	15	Chocolate coconut sauce	48	Chocolate velvet pudding	45
Bars, chocolate caramel	26	Chocolate crunchies	30	Chocolate velvet sauce	49
Biscuits, chocolate dipped	31	Chocolate custard	39	Chocolate zucchini cake	11
Biscuits, Kiwi	32	Chocolate dipped biscuits	31	Chocolate, hot	60
Biscuits, orange chippies	32	Chocolate egg nog	60	Chocolate, hot rich	61
Biscuits, peanut brownies	33	Chocolate fondue	50	Chocolates, easy peppermint creams	57
Brandy balls	54	Chocolate fudge pudding	38	Chocolates, marzipan	57
Bread pudding, chocolate	36	Chocolate fudge sauce	49	Chocolates, sinfully rich	56
Brownies	20	Chocolate glaze	6	Coconut sauce, chocolate	48
Bubble cakes, chocolate	28	Chocolate icecream	44	Crazy cake	17
Cake, Aunt Lucy's mistake	19	Chocolate lamingtons	27	Cream cheese chocolate icing	7
Cake, chocolate apple	10	Chocolate liqueur icing	7	Creamy chocolate sauce	49
Cake, chocolate banana	15	Chocolate lunch box squares	21	Crunchies, chocolate	30
Cake, chocolate orange liqueur	8	Chocolate mousse	43	Custard, chocolate	39
Cake, chocolate upside down	37	Chocolate orange liqueur cake	8	Custard, chocolate pear	40
Cake, chocolate zucchini	11	Chocolate peanut sauce	48	**D**rink, chocolate egg nog	60
Cake, crazy	17	Chocolate pear custard	40	Drink, chocolate spider	61
Cake, Kirsten's chocolate	16	Chocolate sauce, creamy	49	Drink, hot chocolate	60
Cake, Mississippi mud	12	Chocolate shortcake	35	Drink, hot mocha	60
Caramel bars, chocolate	26	Chocolate souffle roll	9	Drink, hot rich chocolate	61
Chocolate Applecake	10	Chocolate spider	61		

Index

Drink, iced mocha	61	**K**irsten's chocolate cake	16	**R**ocky road	29
Easy peppermint creams	57	Kirsten's chocolate roll	18	Roll, chocolate souffle	9
Egg nog, chocolate	60	Kiwi biscuits	32	Roll, Kirsten's chocolate	18
Everyday chocolate icing	6	**L**amingtons, chocolate	27	**S**auce, chocolate coconut	48
Fondue, chocolate	50	Liqueur truffles	55	Sauce, chocolate fudge	49
Fudge pudding, chocolate	38	Little lava rocks	22	Sauce, chocolate peanut	48
Fudge sauce, chocolate	49	**M**arzipan chocolates	57	Sauce, chocolate velvet	49
Fudge square	20	Melt-in-the-mouth fudge	53	Sauce, creamy chocolate	49
Fudge tart, almond & rum	47	Mississippi mud cake	12	Shortcake, chocolate	35
Fudge, melt-in-the-mouth chocolate	53	Mocha icing	6	Sinfully rich chocolates	56
		Mocha truffles	54	Sour cream chocolate icing	7
Glaze, chocolate	6	Mocha, hot	60	Spider, chocolate	61
Hazelnut chocolate pie	46	Mocha, iced	61	Sponge, three minute chocolate	16
Hot chocolate	60	Mousse, chocolate	43	Square, fudge	20
Hot mocha	60	Muffins, chocolate surprise	34	Squares, chocolate lunch box	21
Hot rich chocolate	61	**N**eenish tarts	25	Syrup, chocolate	60
Icecream, chocolate	44	**O**range chippies	32	**T**art, almond and rum fudge	47
Iced mocha	61	**P**eanut brownies	33	Tarts, Neenish	25
Icing, chocolate glaze	6	Peanut sauce, chocolate	48	Three minute chocolate sponge	16
Icing, chocolate liqueur	7	Pear custard, chocolate	40	Truffles, jaffa	54
Icing, cream cheese chocolate	7	Peppermint creams, easy	57	Truffles, liqueur	55
Icing, everyday chocolate	6	Pie, chocolate hazelnut	46	Truffles, mocha	54
Icing, mocha	6	Pudding, chocolate bread	36	Truffles, white chocolate	55
Icing, sour cream chocolate	7	Pudding, chocolate fudge	38	**W**hite chocolate truffles	55
Jaffa truffles	54	Pudding, chocolate velvet	45	**Z**ucchini cake, chocolate	11

Knives by Mail Order

For the past 19 years I have imported my favourite, very sharp kitchen knives from Switzerland. These keep their edges well, are easy to sharpen, and a pleasure to use. These knives are extremely sharp. Please use them with care until you are used to this!

VEGETABLE KNIFE $8.00 Pointed, straight edged, 85mm blade, in a plastic sheath. Useful for peeling vegetables and cutting small objects.

UTILITY KNIFE $9.00 Pointed 103mm blade which slopes back, in a plastic sheath. Use for boning chicken and meat and general kitchen use.

SERRATED KNIFE $9.00 Rounded end, 110mm serrated knife in a plastic sheath. This never needs sharpening, will stay sharp for years, and is unbelievably useful for slicing steak, bread and fresh baking, tomatoes and fruit, etc.

THREE PIECE SET $17.00 Serrated knife (as above), 85mm blade vegetable knife with pointed tip, and (right-handed) potato peeler, all with black dishwasher-proof handles, together in a white plastic pack.

GIFT BOX KNIFE SETS $38.00 Five knives and a (right-handed) potato peeler. Contains straight bladed vegetable knife, blade 85mm; serrated edged vegetable knife, blade 85mm; small utility knife with a pointed tip blade 85mm; small serrated utility 85mm; larger rounded end serrated knife 110mm (same as above). ("Straight edge" means that blade is in line with handle.) Attractive pack.

SERRATED CARVING KNIFE $25.00 Cutting edge 21 cm, overall length 33 cm. Black, moulded dishwasher-proof handle. Cuts beautifully, and does not require sharpening. (Sharpening wears down the serrations.) In sheath.

STEEL $20.00 20 cm blade, 34 cm total length, black dishwasher-proof handle. Produces excellent results.

KNIFE SHARPENER $30.00 This sits on a bench, and is held safely, without slipping, with one hand while you draw a CLEAN knife (of any length) through it with your other hand. Easy to use, with two rotating sharpening disks of synthetic ruby. When knife is held vertically, discs are at ideal angle to sharpen it to a fine point. Dishwasher-proof. Do not use with serrated knives. This is excellent if you have trouble using a steel efficiently.

For each order (any number of knives) please add $3.00 for packing and postage. All prices include GST. These prices apply until the end of 1996.

Please make cheques out to Alison Holst and send with your order to:

Alison Holst Mail Orders
PO Box 17016
Wellington